The Empty House

By

Stacy LaShae

DEDICATION

To my father, Rev. Charles N. Burnside, Sr. (1932-2012), I endeavor to keep your memory alive through Daddy. I miss you and I love you through death.

To my mother, Magdalene Burnside-Clay, thank you for your sharing your empty house idea with me and giving me permission to bring it to life.

To Eric A. Carman Sr., thank you for asking the simple question, "Have you ever thought about writing a children's book?"

In loving memory of: Mary Magdalene Millard, Olivia McClurkin, Alean Grady, and Shawn Christopher Poindexter Jr. Until that Great Day!

For Kamryn

ACKNOWLEDGMENTS

Illustrations by Nicolas Lonprez
Backpack artwork by Eric A. Carman Sr.
Layout by Eric A. Carman Sr.

The sun was shining through the bedroom window as Chloe fastened the buckles on her favorite black shoes. Aunt DiDi had just finished combing Chloe's hair and was now straightening her own hair, carefully adjusting her big black hat. Chloe was confused because she has never gone to church without Mommie.

She didn't quite understand why Mommie didn't come home from the hospital and why she had been gone so many days without kissing her goodnight. Daddy told her that Mommie had died, but she didn't know quite what that meant.

"Chloe, please make sure you do not muss up your hair playing while you wait on us to finish getting dressed. You want to make sure you stay neat and pretty for your Mommie's memorial, don't you?" asked Aunt DiDi.

"Yes ma'am," replied Chloe. She didn't want to muss up her hair for Mommie. Perhaps Mommie would meet them at church. Chloe began to get excited. She really missed Mommie. "I'm going to see Mommie at church," she began to sing as she swung her backpack around joyfully.

Daddy heard Chloe's wonderful song and knew that she didn't quite understand Mommie wasn't coming back. With great concern, he appeared in Chloe's doorway, where she spun her favorite backpack around gleefully. Chloe never went anywhere without her backpack, not even to church.

"Chloe, I need to speak to you before we leave, okay, Princess?"

Chloe looked up at Daddy. She could see he was sad. He missed Mommie too. "We are going to see Mommie at church, Daddy. Why are you sad?" asked Chloe.

"Chloe, we are not going to see Mommie at church, Princess. Let me explain," said Daddy. He picked Chloe up and sat her on the bed. "When I told you Mommie died, what did that mean to you?" he asked.

Chloe looked up at the ceiling and started twirling her fingers through the straps of her backpack. She wasn't quite sure what it meant. All she knew was that Daddy said Mommie had died and she hadn't seen Mommie in several days. Maybe it meant that Mommie was on vacation, so she said, "She's on a vacation?"

Daddy smiled. "No, Princess. She's not on a vacation. When a person dies, that means their body doesn't work anymore," he said.

Chloe was confused. "If her body doesn't work anymore, then how can she come home?"

Daddy pulled her closer and hugged her as he said, "Mommie won't be coming home, Princess."

Chloe began to cry. "But why? Did I do something wrong? Is it because I keep forgetting to pick my backpack off the floor? Tell Mommie I'm sorry. I promise I'll pick my backpack up off the floor," said Chloe with a voice full of remorse.

"Chloe, it's not because of anything you did that Mommie isn't coming home. Let me see if I can help you understand," he said. "You know what a house is right?" he asked.

"Of course I know what a house is. We live in a house, Daddy," said Chloe. "I'm not a baby, you know." Daddy smiled and said, "No Sweetheart, you are not a baby. I apologize for not treating you like a big, smart girl." Daddy continued, "Well, our bodies are like a house. What is inside a house?" he probed.

"Well, there is a lot of stuff in a house," said Chloe. "That is true. Just tell me some special stuff that is inside a house. What are some of Mommie's things?" he asked.

Chloe sat and thought, and thought...and thought.

"Mommie has a lot of shoes and likes to wear pretty dresses. And..." thought Chloe. "She has lots of medicine and wigs," she exclaimed. "Oh! And she has lots of necklaces. A gazillion of them."

Daddy snickered. "So those are the things that belong in Mommie's house. Those are all of the things that are hers," said Daddy. "When we die, it's like moving. Everything that belongs to us is packed up and moved out, leaving the house empty. Mommie's house is empty because her soul went back to God who gave it to her."

"But why?" asked Chloe.

"Mommie was very sick. Most of the time the body can make itself better, like when you have a cold. Remember when you had that sore throat and you got better? The body works very hard to make you better. Sometimes, the body gets very sick and it works very hard to get better, but it gets tired of working so hard so it stops working. That's what happened to Mommie," explained Daddy, trying to keep an even tone although his eyes were very sad.

"Remember when I taught you the story of Adam and how God formed him out of dust?" asked Daddy.

Chloe nodded. She loved the story of Creation and how trees and animals were made.

"What happened after God formed Adam? Was he alive?" asked Daddy.

"No," said Chloe. She was excited because she knew the story well. "God breathed into him the breath of life and man became a living soul," she said excitedly.

"That's right," Daddy responded. "And when we die, our breath goes back to God and our bodies are empty, like a house when we move out," he explained.

Chloe beamed with glee. She was proud of having remembered the story. Then she suddenly became serious and with a voice filled with great concern, she asked, "Will I die when I get sick?"

Daddy didn't want to tell Chloe a fib so he told her the truth. "Your body is very healthy, so you don't have to worry about your body getting tired of fighting anytime soon. You are very healthy," said Daddy.

Sadness came over Chloe when she began to think about how much she missed Mommie, and she began to wonder if Mommie missed her.

Daddy could see her disposition change, so he asked, "How do you feel?"

Chloe fidgeted, shifting in her seat as she thought about how she felt. She waited, twirling the strap on her backpack some more.

Daddy could see she was having difficulty, so he asked her again, "Chloe, sweetie...how do you feel?"

Chloe fidgeted some more and then said, "I feel sad because Mommie might be sad because she misses me."

Daddy gently moved the curl that fell into her eyes and pulled her closer to him, placing his face close to hers. He looked at her and said, "Chloe, Mommie isn't sad because Mommie's body doesn't work anymore. Her body has to work to feel happy, sad, or even angry. We feel happy, sad, or angry because our bodies still work. So don't worry about Mommie. She's no longer feeling pain or sadness."

12

"And do you remember what you learned in church about people who love Jesus?" asked Daddy.

Chloe squinted as she tried to remember what she had learned in Sabbath School. She could remember the story of Mary and Joseph and she could remember the story of Jesus being born. She couldn't recall what she had learned about people who love Jesus and she was embarrassed to tell Daddy she didn't know. So, she put her finger on her chin as she looked up at the ceiling , thinking really hard.

"It's okay if you don't know, Chloe. This is not a test. I'm just trying to understand what we need to talk about, okay Sweetheart?"

"I don't remember, Daddy," said Chloe sadly. She didn't like not knowing stuff because she knew everything.

"Well, there are two things I'm going to tell you about people who love Jesus and die that I want you to remember," Daddy said to Chloe. "Remember when we talked about Jesus coming to take us to heaven one day? When a person dies who loves Jesus, they will get to live with Jesus when He comes back. When Mommie died, she finished all of the work God had for her to do, so she will get a beautiful crown and eternal life. It's a reward, like when you won the ribbon for getting first place in the spelling bee," Daddy explained. "Do you understand?" he asked.

"So you're saying that Jesus is going to come back for Mommie and give her a crown and take her to heaven?" asked Chloe.

"Yes," answered Daddy. "And guess what else? All of the good work she did will live on, even though she had died. People will always remember her kindness, like when she volunteered at the Women's Shelter and when she raised money for cancer and diabetes research. She was a wonderful doctor who saved many lives, and those people are very thankful that she lived to help them. But most importantly, she was a wonderful mother, and you will remember all of the wonderful things she taught you and all of the good times you had with her."

"How does knowing that make you feel?" asked Daddy.

Chloe thought and thought as she looked at the ground. Daddy waited patiently for her answer. A few moments passed and Chloe said, "I feel okay. I'm glad Mommie doesn't hurt anymore and I'm glad she's not sad. But, I'm sad because I miss Mommie."

"I understand, Princess. I miss Mommie too," said Daddy. "She was an amazing woman, very kind and very funny. She was my wife and my best friend. But as long as we remember her, she lives in our hearts."

What is your favorite memory of Mommie?" asked Daddy.

Chloe thought about it. There were so many favorite memories she had of Mommie, such as when Mommie would read her a bedtime story or when they would bake cookies. She also enjoyed coloring with Mommie and playing dolls with Mommie. Then she smiled. "My favorite memory of Mommie is when she would take me for ice cream after I got a good report from Miss Richardson. I never told Mommie, but Miss Richardson gave everyone in the classroom who got good reports a cookie," Chloe said with a smirk.

16

"What is it that you miss most about Mommie?" asked Daddy.

"I miss seeing Mommie the most," replied Chloe. And I miss her singing the most," she added. "And I miss her kissing me goodnight the most," she said, twiddling her fingers and looking at the ground.

"Keeping the memories of Mommie are very important. What are some of the ways you can keep those great memories alive?" asked Daddy.

"I don't know," answered Chloe.

"Okay, well, how about when we return from the memorial service, we start making a scrapbook for you of your favorite pictures of Mommie? When you miss her, you can look at your favorite pictures and favorite things of Mommie. We will create a treasure box, and you can go into our room and take whatever you want that belonged to Mommie and keep it in the treasure box. How does that sound?"

"I would like that very much," said Chloe.

"And when you want to say something to Mommie, write it down, and we'll put it in the treasure box, too. Would that be okay?" asked Daddy.

"Yes, that will be okay." said Chloe.

"It will feel very strange not having Mommie here but we will get through this; all of us together: me, you, and Joshie. We will get through this together okay? When you feel like crying, cry. When you feel like laughing, laugh. When you want to be alone to write to Mommie, just let me know and I'll make sure Joshie doesn't bother you. If you have any questions, just ask me," said Daddy.

"Okay," responded Chloe.

"Do you feel better?" asked Daddy.

"Yes," said Chloe.

Daddy kissed Chloe on the forehead and gives her a big hug. Chloe loved his hugs the most.

"I love you and Mommie loved you, Chloe. Don't ever forget that," said Daddy.

"I love you too, Daddy," replied Chloe.

Daddy sat Chloe down on her bed and turned to the door. "Josh! Please come here a moment. I want to explain to you and Chloe what to expect when we get to the church."

Josh quietly appeared in the doorway and walked into the room, taking a seat on the bed next to Daddy. His face was sullen and his eyes were sad, too.

"Josh, I know this is hard for you son, but we will get through this. I promise." Daddy began to explain, "In a few minutes, we are going to head to the church for Mommie's memorial service. Mommie will be laying in a casket, but her body isn't working so she can't hear you or see you. Do you know what a casket is?" asked Daddy.

Chloe shook her head no. Josh sat quietly, waiting to see what Daddy would say.

"A casket is a soft bed in a decorated box. Mommie's is pink because pink was her favorite color," explained Daddy. "Do you understand?" asked Daddy.

"Kinda," said Josh. Chloe wasn't so sure.

Daddy pulled out his phone and found a picture of a pink casket on the internet.

Both Chloe and Josh looked at it. "I think it's pretty," said Chloe.

"Do you want to see her in the casket? You don't have to see her if you don't want to. It's okay," explained Daddy.

Josh sat quietly for a moment, looking at the ground as he twitched his mouth - he always did that when he was nervous. Still looking at the ground, he said in a voice that cracked, "I would like to say goodbye to Mommie if that is okay."

"Me too," added Chloe.

"Okay," replied Daddy. "That is fine. But if you change your mind, that is okay, too. I want the decision to be yours."

Daddy grabbed Joshie and Chloe's hands, gave them a gentle squeeze of reassurance, and then said, "After the service at the church, we are going to go to the cemetary. The cemetary is where we take people who have died until Jesus returns. When we leave the cemetary, we aren't leaving Mommie, but are leaving her empty house there because her soul is with God. Her soul is what made Mommie alive and it is what makes us alive. Our soul is what helps us hear, taste food, skip, sleep, and even pray. When we die, our soul goes back to God, so don't worry about Mommie. She won't be scared or lonely...or cold. Remember, she doesn't live there anymore."

"Mommie's empty house?" asked Josh in a confused voice.

"Yes, Mommie's empty house," replied Daddy. "If it is okay with you, I would like to take time to explain it to you later. It was a way I explained it to Chloe to help her understand what happened to Mommie. You're a bit older, so your understanding of death is a bit more advanced," Daddy winked at Joshie.

"Got it," said Josh.

Aunt DiDi suddenly reappeared in the doorway. "Michael, the funeral car is here for us," she said calmly.

"Thank you," replied Daddy. He stood up and turned to look at Chloe and Josh. "It's time to go. Remember, I am here for you if you ever want to talk."

They all walked outside towards the big black car.
Chloe looked up at the sky, which was clear blue
with a bright and beautiful sun. She could
hear the birds singing a beautiful song and it
made her smile. "What a pretty day to go see an
empty house," she told Daddy. She thought about
Creation and how God made the birds and the
sun. She smiled, knowing Mommie's soul was
with God.

"Then I saw a new Heaven and a new Earth, for old Heaven and the old Earth had disappeared. And the sea was also gone. And I saw the holy city, the new Jerusalem, coming down from God out of Heaven like a bride beautifully dressed for her husband.

I heard a loud shout from the throne, saying, 'Look, God's home is now among His people! He will live with them, and they will be His people. God himself will be with them. He will wipe every tear from their eyes, and there will be no more death or sorrow or crying or pain. All these things are gone forever.'"

-Revelation 21:1-5 (NLT)

www.ingramcontent.com/pod-product-compliance
Lightning Source LLC
Chambersburg PA
CBHW041239040426
42445CB00004B/79